## Ken-ichi Sakura

A big building has gone up next to my studio, cutting off all the daylight. I must get exposure to the sun! So I'm looking for a new place that gets plenty of morning light. It sure is tough to find a comfortable workplace.

(I don't need to do any more trash jokes, right?)

Ken-ichi Sakura's manga debut was *Fabre Tanteiki*, which was published in a special edition of *Monthly Shonen Jump* in 2000. Serialization of *Dragon Drive* began in the March 2001 issue of *Monthly Shonen Jump* and the hugely successful series has inspired video games and an animated TV show. Sakura's latest title, *Kotokuri*, began running in the March 2006 issue of *Monthly Shonen Jump*. *Dragon Drive* and *Kotokuri* have both become tremendously popular in Japan because of Sakura's unique sense of humor and dynamic portrayal of feisty teen characters.

# DRAGON DRIVE

DRAGON DRIVE
VOLUME 9

The SHONEN JUMP Manga Edition

STORY AND ART BY
**KEN-ICHI SAKURA**

Translation/Martin Hunt, HC Language Solutions, Inc.
English Adaptation/Ian Reid, HC Language Solutions, Inc.
Touch-up Art & Lettering/Jim Keefe
Cover Design/Sam Elzway
Interior Design/Mark Griffin
Editor/Shaenon K. Garrity

Editor in Chief, Books/Alvin Lu
Editor in Chief, Magazines/Marc Weidenbaum
VP of Publishing Licensing/Rika Inouye
VP of Sales/Gonzalo Ferreyra
Sr. VP of Marketing/Liza Coppola
Publisher/Hyoe Narita



Printed in the U.S.A.

Published by VIZ Media, LLC
P.O. Box 77010
San Francisco, CA 94107

SHONEN JUMP Manga Edition
10 9 8 7 6 5 4 3 2 1
First printing, August 2008

THE WORLD'S MOST POPULAR MANGA

www.shonenjump.com

SHONEN JUMP MANGA EDITION

# DRAGON DRIVE

Vol. 9

RESHUFFLE

# CHARACTERS

## Takumi Yukino

A LAID-BACK KID WHO GETS INTO DRAGON DRIVE AFTER RECEIVING A RAIKOO CARD. HE'S GOT A TOUGH OLDER SISTER.

## Raikoo

TAKUMI'S DRAGON. HE'S LOST HIS MEMORIES OF HIS LIFE BEFORE HE MET TAKUMI.

AN EXPERIENCED DRAGON DRIVE PLAYER WHO SHOWS TAKUMI THE ROPES.

## Master

THE MANAGER OF GAME SHOP KOIZUMI. HE KNOWS AGENT L.

## Mysterious Old Man

THE GUY WHO GAVE TAKUMI HIS RAIKOO CARD.

## STORY

A GAME CALLED DRAGON DRIVE IS BECOMING WILDLY POPULAR WITH KIDS ALL OVER THE WORLD. ONE DAY, TAKUMI YUKINO RECEIVES A DECK OF D.D. CARDS FROM A MYSTERIOUS OLD MAN. EVEN THOUGH HIS SISTER HAS FORBIDDEN HIM TO PLAY, TAKUMI ENTERS A LOCAL D.D. TOURNAMENT, UNABLE TO IGNORE HIS NEW THIRST FOR EXCITEMENT.

FOR HIS FIRST MATCH, TAKUMI ACCIDENTALLY ENTERS THE TOURNAMENT FINALS, FACING AN EXPERIENCED PLAYER. EVEN THOUGH HE'S NEVER PLAYED BEFORE, THE STRENGTH OF RAIKOO HELPS HIM WIN. AT GAME SHOP KOIZUMI, HE BEGINS TRAINING FOR THE UPCOMING NATIONAL TOURNAMENT.

ONE NIGHT, TAKUMI HAS A STRANGE DREAM. HE'S TOLD THAT TO AWAKEN THE TRUE RAIKOO FROM AMONG THE 99 RAIKOO CARDS, ALL THE RAIKOOS MUST FIGHT EACH OTHER. THE DREAM WORRIES TAKUMI, BUT HE HEADS FOR THE NATIONAL TOURNAMENT ANYWAY, HOPING THAT IT WILL HELP RESTORE RAIKOO'S LOST MEMORIES...

Vol. 9 RESHUFFLE

# CONTENTS



DRAGON DRIVE

AT LAST THE NATIONAL TOURNAMENT HAS BEGUN!
IT'LL BE TOUGH FOR A TOTAL BEGINNER LIKE ME TO FIGHT IN THIS TOURNAMENT...
...BUT THAT'S NOT MY ONLY HEADACHE.
THE OLD MAN WHO GAVE ME MY D.D. CARDS...
...TOLD ME THAT THE RAIKOO MASTERS MUST MAKE THEIR RAIKOOS FIGHT...
...TO AWAKEN THE TRUE RAIKOO.
OH, WELL... I GUESS I'VE GOTTA JUST GO FOR IT!
4th turn Rival

FIGHT! FIGHT!!
BAM
LISTEN UP! I'M GONNA WIN, WIN, WIN!
MY DRAGON'S GONNA BE THE STRONGEST!
I CAN'T LOSE!!
Raikoo Master
Maria Tsukimi

YOU'RE A RAIKOO MASTER, TOO, RIGHT?
WELL, SAME HERE!
I CAN'T LOSE, EITHER !!
IF IT'LL HELP GET RAIKOO'S MEMORY BACK...
...I'LL FIGHT YOU!
HMPH
TA-KUMI!
SNIFFLE

YAAAY
THIS IS AMAZING! FIGHTS BETWEEN RAIKOOS ARE BREAKING OUT ALL OVER!
SO MANY RAI-KOOS!
WHAT ON **EARTH** IS OUR DEVELOP-MENT DEPARTMENT THINKING?
OH, NO!! DOES THIS MEAN RAIKOO IS THE HOT NEW THING...
...AND I'M THE ONLY ONE WHO'S BEEN LEFT BEHIND?
WHY, JUST THIS MORNING...
EEP
IT'S THE OLD LADY FROM DRAGON DRIVE!
OLD?
THAT WAS A CRUEL BLOW...
OWW
OWW
THAT CHICK LOOKS LIKE SHE'S IN PAIN.
I BET HER TUMMY'S COLD IN THOSE CLOTHES...

READ THIS WAY
SPEAKING OF PAIN, WHAT'S UP WITH TAKUMI'S FIGHT?
HE'S ACTING SO WEIRD.
YEEK
IS HE TRYING OR NOT?
I REALLY DON'T GET THAT GUY...
SIGH
I...
...THINK TAKUMI...
...IS LIKE A WILLOW TREE.
A WHAT?
?

RRRM
KLAK
KLAK
AN ATTACK BY MARIA TSUKIMI!! SHE'S WAY OFF TARGET, BUT WHAT AMAZING POWER!!
FWOOM

HOW ABOUT THAT WIDE INTER-SECTION?
LOOKS GOOD!
RIGHT! I'M GOING DOWN!
FWOOM
!
A PERSON ?!
RAIKOO, NO! THERE'S SOMEONE BELOW US!!
WHAT?
KRUNCH

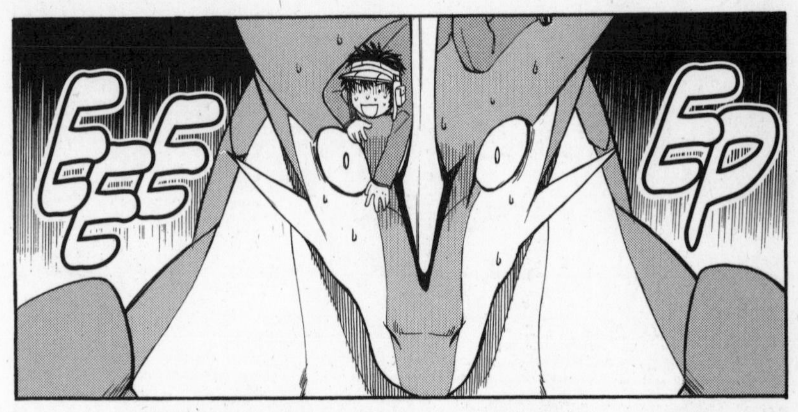
EEEE
EP

DID YOU... SQUASH HIM?
I...I DON'T KNOW ...
COULD YOU, ER, CHECK FOR ME?
I'M AFRAID TO LOOK DOWN!!
BRR
BRR
BRR

THIS COULD SCAR ME FOR LIFE...
SHOOOOP
AHA!
IT'S OKAY! YOU JUST MISSED HIM!
WHAT A RELIEF!!

READ THIS WAY

I DON'T THINK HE'S INJURED. IN FACT...
HA HA HA
...HE'S ASLEEP! TALK ABOUT RELAXED ...
AT LEAST HE'S NOT UPSET.
ZZZ
ZZZ

WE HAVE NO TIME FOR THIS, TAKUMI.
LET'S WAKE HIM BEFORE THAT GIRL CATCHES UP TO US.
ROGER.

HEY, WAKE UP. ARE YOU OKAY?
SNORT

THIS ISN'T THE BEST PLACE FOR A NAP.
UGH...I NODDED OFF.

IT WAS JUST ...
...TOO BORING.
HUH?

HUP!

AH.
WAAAA

LOOOM
WHAT'S UP?
HE'S HUGE !!

READ THIS WAY

KABOOM
HEY HEY HEY!!
CRUNCH
OMM

CRU
NCH
CH
I WON'T LET YOU GET AWAY!!
BOOM

ROOOAR
WAH WAH
SHE'S CHARGING THROUGH THE BUILDINGS AS IF THEY WEREN'T THERE!! THAT'S ONE POWERFUL GIRL!!
OKAY, SUCKERS!
GIVE IT UP FOR MY RAIKOO!
UM... WE'LL FIGHT HERE!
RIGHT!
IT'S GONNA GET DANGEROUS, BRO! YOU'D BETTER GET OUT OF HERE!
YAWN
I'LL FIND SOMEWHERE ELSE TO SLEEP.
WEIRD.
Tp Tp Tp Tp

WAIT RIGHT THERE!!
WHAT?
YOU...
HA HA HA!
I'D FORGET THE FACES OF MY OWN PARENTS BEFORE I'D FORGET YOURS...
...TARO OTO-HIME!!
HM? SOMEBODY CALL?
DON'T MOVE A MUSCLE!
I'VE COME ALL THIS WAY TO GET REVENGE ON YOU!!
I'LL KILL YOU!
HISSS
R... REVENGE!?
HAVE WE MET?

SOB
YOU CHEWED MY HEART UP AND SPAT IT OUT!!
WHOA
YOU ASKED ME OUT ON A DATE...
GRR
...THEN DUMPED ME IN UNDER 30 MINUTES!
OH...

READ THIS WAY

LET'S SPLIT UP.

...I GOT BORED.

SO I DUMPED HER.

CLANG

CLANG!

ER...THAT WAS KINDA COLD. SHOULDN'T YOU APOLOGIZE?

COLD?

HMM... YEAH...

I GUESS...

...I'M JUST NOT A NICE GUY.

I ONLY JUDGE THINGS ON WHETHER THEY'RE ***INTERESTING*** OR ***BORING.***

I HATE BEING BORED.

WHAT A PECULIAR CHARACTER.

YEAH, HE'S A SUPERFREAK.

BUT I GUESS IT WAS WRONG TO HURT HER.

READ THIS WAY

PENMARUN MATERIALIZED!!
WATER
PENMARUN
LV.1
AP 1900
Pow 1
AWW!
IT'S CUTE...
GYUU
GIMME YOUR BEST SHOT!
BRING IT!
I'LL LET YOU HAVE THE FIRST MOVE.
PASS.
HUH?
DON'T UNDER-ESTIMATE ME!!
ZOOM

READ THIS WAY

THWOK
SHWEE

NEXT.

PASS.
BOOM
SUIKOO MATERIALIZED!
WATER SUIKOO
LV.1 AP 1500 0

PALIGHT MATERIALIZED!!

LIGHT
PALIGHT
LV.1 AP 2600 Pow 0

ARE YOU TAKING THIS SERIOUSLY?

I'VE BEEN SUM-MONED!
ACK... DON'T HURT ME!
YOU'RE GOING DOWN!!
PASS.
ARRGH!
KRUMP
!

HUH?
STOP IT!
QUIT PICKING ON DEFENSELESS OPPONENTS!!
GRRR!
WHAT ARE YOU DOING?
WHAM
IF YOU GET IN THE WAY, I'LL TAKE YOU DOWN TOO!!
UGH!

DON'T GIVE UP, TARO!!
DON'T SULK JUST BECAUSE YOU CAN'T GET THE CARDS YOU WANT OUT OF YOUR DECK.
DO YOUR BEST WITH THE DRAGONS YOU GOT!!
THAT'S NOT WHAT THIS GUY'S LIKE!
HUH?
DON'T GET YOUR KNICKERS IN A KNOT.
I'M KILLING THEM OFF ON PURPOSE.
THEY'RE WEAK, BORING CARDS.

WHAT ARE YOU SAYING?
IT'S YOUR JOB TO MAKE THEM INTERESTING!
YOU! WHAT'S YOUR SPECIAL ATTACK?
HUH? ME?
I... I CAN GLOW.
I CAN GLOW REALLY BRIGHT!
THESE BULBS ON MY WINGS LIGHT UP!
THAT'S SWEET!
...

READ THIS WAY

WHAT-EVER! LET'S SEE YOU GLOW!

ROAR

...

YEAH, THAT'S IT.

ROAR

WHAT NEXT?

LET ME SEE...

HEY.

HANG ON.

CAN YOU...

...SPEAK TO DRAGONS?!

TIME TO PLUCK YOU BALD!!
SWOOP
PALIGHT!! GO!
SUGGESTIVE HYPNOTISM!!
WOOM
IT... IT'S NO GOOD!
HE HAS TO GLOW BRIGHTER THAN THAT!!
!
RAIKOO! WE'LL ATTACK, TOO!!

DAIRAIKA!!*
*MASSIVE LIGHTNING BOLT

DOOOOOM

NICE AIM, LOSER!!
!!
I GET IT!!
PALIGHT!!
SHOOM

SHING
SHOOF
EEEEEK!!
SHOOF
SHOOF

TWINKLE
I'M TOTALLY DAZZLED! I CAN'T SEE!
TWINKLE
TWINKLE

ARRGH... MY EYES!!
UGH!!
BRR
BRR
OOGLE BOOGLE

MARIA!
IF I WIN...

...I WANT YOU...
...TO FORGIVE ME.
HEH

BAKURENKOU*
*RAGING BLAST
FOOMM
WILDBURST!!

BLAMA
TARO'S COMBO IS ON TARGET!!
EEEK! NO WAY!!
GAME OVER, MS. TSU-KIMI!!
SHO OMM

WAY TO GO, TAKUMI!
YAY
HE USED THE GLASS FROM THE BUILDING TO INCREASE THE LIGHT REFLECTION!!
HE SEEMS LIKE A TOTAL IDIOT...
...BUT MAYBE HE'S KINDA SMART.
YAY
YAY

I TOLD YOU. JUST LIKE A WILLOW TREE.
HE LETS HIMSELF BEND IN THE WIND.

AT FIRST GLANCE, HE LOOKS WEAK...
...BUT HE DOESN'T SNAP UNDER PRESSURE.

READ THIS WAY

TAKUMI!!

TWO OF THEM!

NOT FRIENDS OF YOURS, I PRESUME.

ER... NO.

THAT IS...

I'LL TAKE OUT THE TRASH.

HUH?

PALIGHT IS DISPELLED.
WHOA!
HE'S COMING THIS WAY!!

VOOM
SWP

SWOOSH

DUDE! WE'RE ONLY INTERESTED IN THE LITTLE GUY!

W... WE DIDN'T COME TO START NOTHIN' WITH YOU!!

I HATE BOREDOM.

WATER
RAIKOO: ANIMA
LV.–
AP
Pow
TARO... YOU'RE ...

...A RAIKOO MASTER, TOO!!
YUP. SHALL WE BEGIN?

BY NAGI

Double Act?
MY HEAD'S THROB-BING...
I FEEL STRANGE ...
THIS LOOKS FAMILIAR ...
GRR
BRR
BRR
OH, YEAH!
BE QUIET!
EEP EEP
AHA
IT'S LIKE WHEN MY CAT HAD KITTENS !!
RAIKOO MUST BE PREG-NANT!
YOU'VE GOTTA FIGHT ME!
NO... NOT YET...
RAIKOO'S A MOMMY !!
HE'S IN A DELI-CATE CONDI-TION!
TAKUMI!!
WHAT A KIND HEART YOU HAVE!
MAJOR MIS-UNDER-STAND-ING.
SNIFF
TEARS OF JOY.

THE FIRST ROUND OF THE DRAGON DRIVE NATIONAL TOURNAMENT IS A MASSIVE BATTLE ROYALE!!
YAAAAAY
ONLY 50 CAN ADVANCE TO THE SECOND ROUND! FIGHT AS HARD AS YOU CAN!!

AREN'T THERE A LOT OF RAIKOOS IN THIS TOURNAMENT?
WHAT? DON'T YOU KNOW?
ERK!
RAIKOOS ARE THE HOT NEW THING!!
YOU'RE BEHIND THE TIMES!

I KNOW WHAT'S HIP!
WHO'S AN OLD LADY NOW?
UH, WHAT?
IS THAT SO?
SHE'S JUST MAKING IT UP...

5th turn Awakening
TARO... YOU'RE ...
...A RAIKOO MASTER, TOO!!

YUP.
SHALL WE
BEGIN?

UGH!
THWAK
RAI-KOO!!
BLUB
FOOSH

TAKUMI!
THWAK
OW!
GRRRM
GET WITH THE PROGRAM.
IF YOU DON'T MAKE THIS *FUN*...
...I'M GONNA GET BORED.

SUICHUKA!!*

*METEOR PILLAR FLOWER

BOOM

ARRGH!

KABOOM

KABOOM

HEH
THIS GUY...
WHY'RE YOU RUNNING, TAKUMI?
GIVE THAT DUDE...
...AN HONEST BUTT-KICKING!
FIGHT HIM!!
HE'S NOT GOING TO LET US GO.
YEAH, YOU'RE RIGHT!
OKAY, FINE!
I'LL FIGHT!!

SHOOOOOM
WSH
WSH
WHOA!
HE MOVES SO FAST I CAN'T SEE HIM!!

HYOUJINRAN!!*

*HAIL BLADE STORM

ARRGH!
KABOOM
URRGH!
HE'S STRONG.
I THINK THIS ONE IS CALLED ANIMA...

READ THIS WAY

BRR
BRR
HFF
HFF

TAKUMI'S NOT READY...

...TO FIGHT HIM!

READ THIS WAY

PASS !!

READ THIS WAY

YOU'RE MAKING ME YAWN...
SH

...
TAKUMI.
TA-
KU-
MI
!!
FWOOOO

DAIRYUUKA!!*
*GREAT FLOWING FLOWER

READ THIS WAY

BOOM

FWUMP

AS LONG AS YOU'RE NOT HURT...

...EVERYTHING'S OKAY...

GRP

RAIKOOO!!

CRUNCH
CRUNCH
ERKK
TARO!!

WHAT'S WRONG, TAKUMI?
WHY'RE YOU ALL JITTERY?
GRANDPA!
ARE YOU SCARED OF THE DOG?
RUFF RUFF
EEEEK!
WAAAH!
MAN UP, BOY.
STAY CALM.
IF YOU JUST KEEP YOUR HEAD, THERE'S NOTHING TO FEAR.
GRRRR
CHOMP

READ THIS WAY
HA HA HA HA!
WAAAH!
GETTING BITTEN WASN'T SO BAD. DRY YOUR EYES.

LISTEN, TAKUMI. THE SCARIEST THING OF ALL...
...IS LOSING CONTROL OF YOURSELF.

IF YOU ***PANIC,*** YOU CAN'T SEE THINGS THAT'RE RIGHT IN FRONT OF YOUR EYES.
IT'S IMPORTANT NOT TO CLOSE THE EYES IN YOUR ***HEART.***

LET ME GIVE YOU SOME ADVICE.
A LITTLE SPELL TO HELP YOU OPEN YOUR HEART.

SHWP

FIRST, CLOSE YOUR EYES.

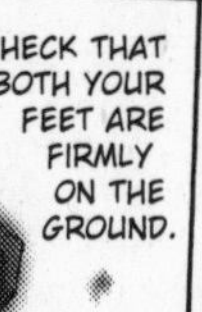

READ THIS WAY

CLOMP

KRRRK

RAIKOO STOOD UP!
HE'S GOT GOOD EYES...

YOU **ARE** INTERESTING, TAKUMI!

I'M GONNA GIVE YOU EVERYTHING I'VE GOT!!

GRRRRM

READ THIS WAY

LET'S USE THIS CARD.
Effect
OPTION CARD

BUT THAT'S ...

HE'S GOING TO USE "MASTERY OF ANTICI-PATION."

HE WANTS TO DEFLECT TARO'S ATTACK!
THERE'S NO ***WAY*** HE CAN DO THAT!

ONLY PLAYERS WHO CAN PREDICT THEIR OPPONENTS' ATTACKS CAN USE THAT CARD!
IF HE GETS IT WRONG, THE DAMAGE WILL BE ***DOUBLED!***

TAKUMI, I ALWAYS TRUST YOUR INSTRUCTIONS.
I'M READY TO PUT ALL MY POWER INTO THIS!!

LET'S DO IT, RAI-KOO!!
RRM
LAM

GR
SHING
B
THE BATTLE STARTS HERE!!

RGRM
GENBYOU-RYUUGEKI!!*
SHLUP
*ILLUSIONARY ICE DRAGON ATTACK
AS LONG AS YOU DON'T CLOSE THE EYES IN YOUR HEART...
...YOU'LL BE ABLE TO SEE EVERYTHING.
I'M GONNA ANTICIPATE THE ATTACK...
...JUST AS IT HITS!!

READ THIS WAY
NOW!!
HW
P
RAIKOOO!!
RAAARGH!!

DARAIKA!!

KABOOM

NICE ONE!

OPTION CARD

Effect Mastery of Anticipation

MASTERY OF ANTICIPATION

READ THIS WAY

VMM MMMMM MMM
END OF ROUND ONE! ALL THE SURVIVING D-MASTERS...
...QUALIFY FOR THE SECOND ROUND! CONGRATULATIONS!!
YAY
YAY
THAT GUY TARO...
...LET TAKUMI GO.
TAKUMI YUKINO...
...QUALIFIES FOR ROUND TWO.
HFF HFF

READ THIS WAY
"LET HIM GO"?
YOU DON'T GET IT, DO YOU?
TAKUMI WAS ABOUT TO PULL OUT A "COUNTER SPELL" CARD...
...TO DEFLECT MY ATTACK.
IF WE'D KEPT FIGHTING, I WOULD'VE GOTTEN **WASTED.**
HEH.
YEAH...
...THIS IS GETTING FUN.

Effect
OPTION CARD
Mastery of Anticipation

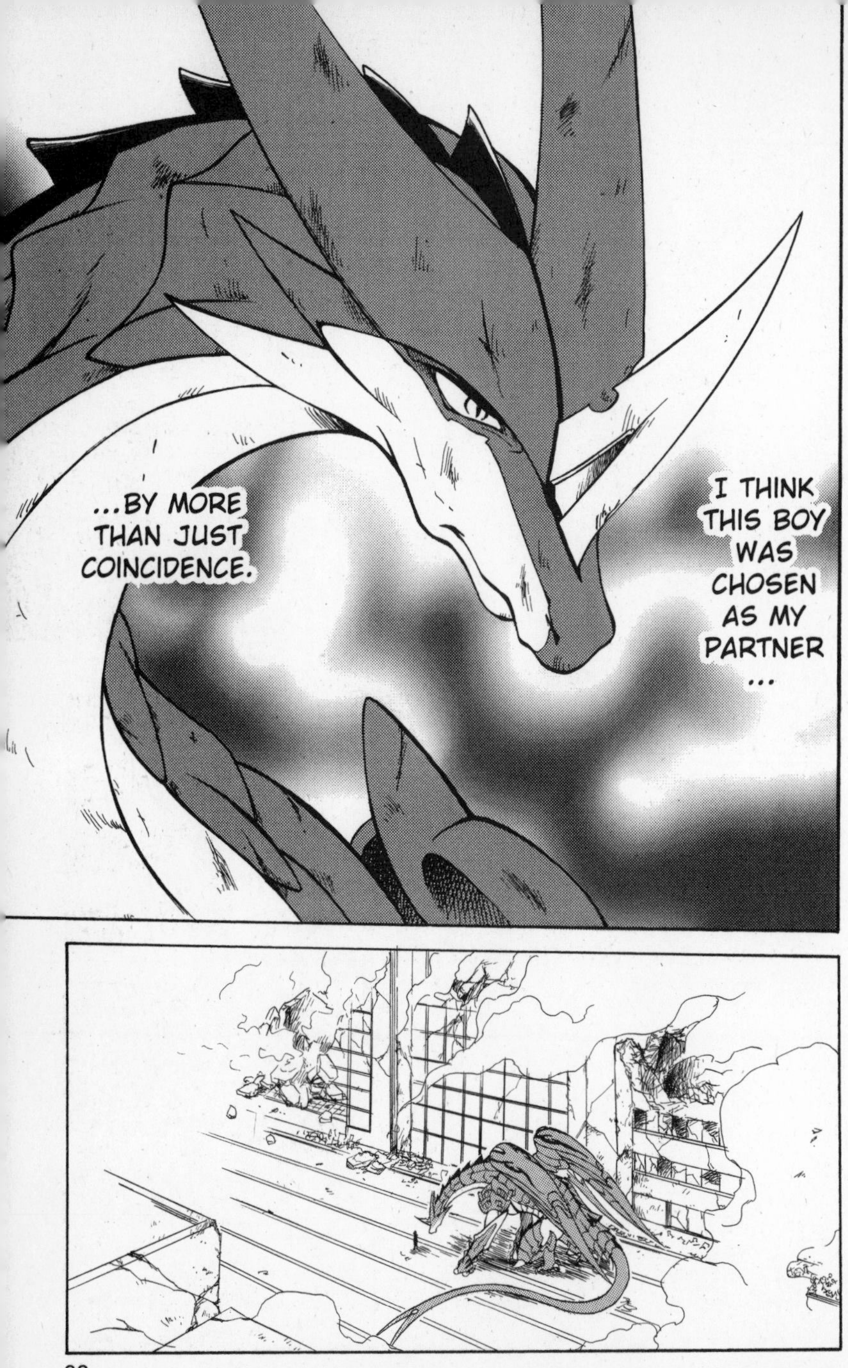

I THINK THIS BOY WAS CHOSEN AS MY PARTNER ...

...BY MORE THAN JUST COINCIDENCE.

BY NAGI

A Long Time
YOU DID WELL...
...TO ENDURE MY LONG TRAINING.
IT WAS ONLY THREE DAYS!
YEAH...
YOU HARDLY DID ANYTHING.
THAT'S RIGHT.
IN THAT CASE...
GLARE
...YOU DID WELL TO ENDURE ME!!
AWW. YOU'RE SCARY, BUT YOU'RE AN OKAY DUDE.
HA HA HA
DON'T JUDGE A BOOK BY ITS COVER.
WHAT ARE YOU BABBLING ABOUT? I WAS TALKING TO TAKUMI!
?

BOOM

IT'S THE EVENT YOU'VE BEEN WAITING FOR! THE SECOND ROUND OF THE NATIONAL TOURNAMENT IS A ***ONE-ON-ONE BATTLE!!***

WAAH

WAAAH

# 6th turn Pride

BWAA
TAKUMI'S RIGHT AT THE BACK.
HE'S GOT THOSE DEAD EYES AGAIN. IS HE OKAY?

...

KRRRK
RAIKOO!!
GRP

READ THIS WAY

WAAH WAAHH

OH, *YOU.*

I DIDN'T EXPECT THE LEADER OF THE ***DAICHI GANG*** TO SHOW UP SOLO.

YOU DON'T USUALLY DO OFFICIAL TOURNAMENTS.

**BUNROKU'S HELMET READS "AZUMA." HIS T-SHIRT READS "CASTLE."*

I'M HERE BECAUSE I HEARD YOU WERE FIGHTING.
I'VE GOT A SCORE TO SETTLE WITH YOU, TARO OTOHIME!
Daichi Gang Leader
Bunroku Azuma
WELL, SHUCKS.
I DON'T REALLY WANT TO PUT ALL MY CARDS ON THE TABLE...
OKAY, THE FIRST DRAW IS DECIDED!
THESE ARE THE PLAYERS!
THE FIRST GAME
TAKUMI YUKINO
VS
BUNNROKU AZUMA
AWW, THERE GOES THE GUY I WAS AFTER...
TAKUMI ...
... YUKINO?
YAY YA

READ THIS WAY

I, BUNROKU AZUMA, HAVE A GRAND DREAM!
I WILL BUILD A CASTLE AND LIVE OUT MY DAYS SURROUNDED BY ANIMALS AND FRIENDS! THAT'S ALL! THANK YOU!!

HUH?
WHOA!
WAH WAH
THAT HAS NOTHING TO DO WITH DRAGON DRIVE!!
BIG DREAMS, SMALL BODY! THE UNSTOPPABLE BUNROKU, FOLKS!
REMEMBER THAT.
HMPH

OKAY! NEXT UP: HE LOOKS SPACEY, BUT HE'S GOT SKILLS!
LET'S HEAR IT FOR TAKUMI YUKINO!
...
BWOOOO

READ THIS WAY

I'M ...
...FORFEITING THIS TOURNAMENT.

WHAAAAT?!

THANK YOU!
SO LONG!

WAIT !!
ZOOOOM
YOU CAN'T DO THAT!
WHAT THE DING-DONG?
TA-KUMI!
I WON'T LET YOU!!
HE'S TOTALLY IGNORING ME...
HEH HEH HEH ...
SO THAT'S HIS PLAN.
WELL, IF TAKUMI'S NOT PLAYING, THIS'LL BE A SNORE.
I'M GOING HOME, TOO.
TARO. WHO IS THAT GUY?

YOU'LL KNOW IF YOU FIGHT HIM.
TAKUMI YUKINO...
HE'S INTERESTING.
EVERY-BODY'S QUITTING.
I'M GOING, TOO.
EEEK!
WHAT'S GOING ON?
IT'S JUST GETTING TO THE GOOD PART!!
EXIT
WHAT'S HAPPENING?

ONE WEEK LATER...

...TAKUMI HAS DISAPPEARED.

GEEZ!

IT WINDS ME UP JUST *THINKING* ABOUT IT!

READ THIS WAY

THE DAICHI GANG ...
...IS FULLY ASSEMBLED!!

HOLD IT!
BAM
YOU GUYS ARE TALKING TRASH!!
WHO IS THIS PUNK?
BUTT OUT, LOSER.
SNAP

BOOM

D-Zone

HAH!

WHAT'S UP? CAN'T HIT ME?

WIND GUST ATTACKER
LV.2 AP 1500 Pow 0

FUGA!!*
*WIND FANG
BAM
THWAP

ZANKUI!!*

*CUTTING WIND OF POWER

SPLAT SPLAT

DON'T UNDER-ESTIMATE ME!

LOSERS!!

EARTH HINDER
LV.3 AP 3400 Pow 1

YOU'RE THE ONE...

...UNDER-ESTIMATING US.

SHOOM
NIN
HIS DRAGON VANISHED!
MUONSASSHU!!*
*SILENT SLAYER

READ THIS WAY

I CAN'T SEE IT!!
WHERE'S THE ATTACK COMING FROM?
BLAM
BLAM
YOU CAN'T SEE THROUGH HINDER'S TECHNIQUES...
...CAN YOU, BROOM-HEAD?
OOOG

WHOA!
WHAT'S HAPPEN-ING?
WAAAH

BLAM

I'LL SHOW YOU MY TRICK.
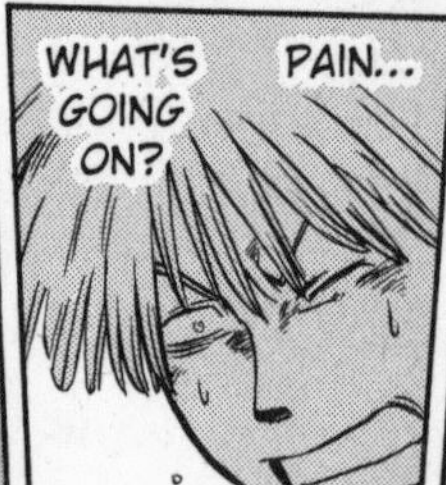
PAIN...
WHAT'S GOING ON?

UGH.

OH! LOOK!!

HE WAS CAMOUFLAGED AGAINST THE BACK-GROUND...
...MAKING HIMSELF LOOK INVISIBLE !!
HRK HRK HRK

I...I COULDN'T SEE ANYTHING!

JUST AS I THOUGHT. PLAYERS WHO HANG AROUND THE GAME CENTERS ARE ***LAME.***

THIS IS NO CHALLENGE AT ALL.

I'M TA-KUMI.

DID YOU WANT SOME-THING?

!

WHY'D YOU HAVE TO TURN UP *NOW*?

DO YOU REMEMBER ME, TAKUMI YUKINO?

HAVE WE MET?

?

I THINK...

...THE MOST ANNOYING THING IN THE WORLD...

...IS BEING *IG-NORED*-!!

TAKE THIS!

NINSATSU!!

BAM

!

MUONSASSHU!!
SWOOSH
HOW'S THIS, TAKUMI?
SWOOSH
CAN YOU SEE ME?

SHOOM
WHOA! LOOK OUT!
TA-KUMI!
SWSHSH
WHAT ?!
SWOOP
CHOMP

KRUNCH
UGH...
...
WOOW
HE SAW RIGHT THROUGH THE TECHNIQUE!!
COOL!!
JUST GO HOME, TAKUMI!
OUT THE WAY! OUT THE WAY!
COOL IT, KENJI.
HEY... WHOA, WHOA.
I'M GONNA TAKE HIM OUT MYSELF!!
I'M NOT GONNA LEAVE HIM TO SOME COWARD WHO TURNED TAIL AND RAN!!
THERE'S NO WAY I CAN FORGIVE YOU!
FZZZT
THAT'S NOT THE WAY I RAISED YOU...

KENJI KOTO: PROGRAM TERMI-NATED.
VRRRM

KENJI, YOU'RE EXPELLED FOR BEING TOO NOISY.
HUH?
STEP OFF, YOU UGLY GORILLA !!

JUST SHUT UP.
IF YOU WANT TO KNOW WHAT TAKUMI HAS BEEN DOING FOR THE PAST WEEK...
...JUST WATCH HIM WELL.

THE PAST WEEK?

YEAH.
ON THE DAY HE FORFEITED THE NATIONAL TOURNA-MENT...

KOIZUMI
GAME SHOP
WHAT?
YOU WANT TO SLEEP AT MY STORE FOR A WEEK?
ER... MASTER, DO YOU LIKE PIGS?
PIGS?
I GUESS THEY'RE OKAY.
GREAT. HERE'S MY RENT.
A PIGGY BANK ...
FEEL FREE TO BREAK IT OPEN.
CHING
THAT TOURNAMENT TODAY...
WHY DID YOU FORFEIT?

WERE YOU SCARED TO LOSE?
NO!
IF YOU HAVE A REASON, TELL ME.
IF YOU DON'T, I'M SENDING YOU HOME.
I...

I WANTED TO GIVE 100 PERCENT AGAINST THOSE PEOPLE.
BUT I STILL DON'T HAVE ENOUGH EXPERIENCE OR KNOWLEDGE.
I FIGURED I COULD JOIN A TOURNA-MENT ANY OLD TIME...
...BUT NOW IT'S MORE IMPORTANT FOR ME TO ***TRAIN.***
IF I CAN GET STRONGER IN TIME FOR THE NEXT TOURNAMENT...
...IT'LL BE ***WAY*** MORE THRILLING TO COMPETE!

READ THIS WAY

NOT BAD.
YOUR RAIKOO'S STRONGER THAN I THOUGHT.

BUT LET ME SHOW YOU WHAT I CAN DO.
SWSH
SWSH
WHIRR WHIRR

TRY DODGING *THIS* ONE!!

PHOOOM

SANGE-TSUJIN!!*

*MOONSTRIKE

PHOOOO OM

Field Card:
Land of the Black Cloud

RRM RRM

IS RAIKOO **ABSORBING THE LIGHTNING?**
HE'S **WEARING** THE LIGHTNING.
THIS IS HIS TRUE FORM!

ROOAR

READ
THIS
WAY

PHOOOOOOM
OKAY, WHAT'RE YOU GONNA DO?

LET'S GO, RAI-KOO!

FOOOM

BLAM
BLAM

READ THIS WAY
FWSH
NUTS! MY REACTION WAS TOO SLOW!
I CAN'T HESI-TATE!
SHOOOM
DEFENSIVE SHIELD
ACTIVATED!!
OPTION CARD
Defensive Shield
THOONK

NO ...
IT'S TOO POWER-FUL...

THE SHIELD ...

... WON'T HOLD!

READ THIS WAY

FWAM

FSSTT

WH...
WHAT HAPPENED?

FWUMP

THIS GUY'S AMAZING!
NO WONDER HE CAUGHT TARO'S ATTENTION!

WAY TO GO, TAKUMI!
THAT BUNROKU KID MUST BE GOOD TO SURVIVE THAT ATTACK...
NOW THINGS ARE GETTING INTEREST-ING!!

BY NAGI

Hidden Talent
I HEAR THERE ARE SOME NEW CARDS AT KOIZUMI TODAY.
RIGHT?
WHAT-EVER...
YEAH, BUT THEY'RE NOT D.D. CARDS.
YOU'RE RIGHT! THEY'RE DIFFERENT!
AND I WAS GOING TO SPEND MY SAVINGS...
NEW RELEASE !!
FLORAL BEAUTY
THE ULTIMATE GIRLIE GAME! MEN CAN'T RESIST THIS ONE! FEATURING 52 CUTE GIRLS!
PLEASE BUY!
AND A HAND-DRAWN FLYER... IT'S A LABOR OF LOVE!
I DREW IT. IS THERE A PROBLEM?
THIS?
I'LL DRAW ONE FOR YOU, TOO.
HERE.
TA
DA
AH...
NO-WHERE TO RUN.
UGH...

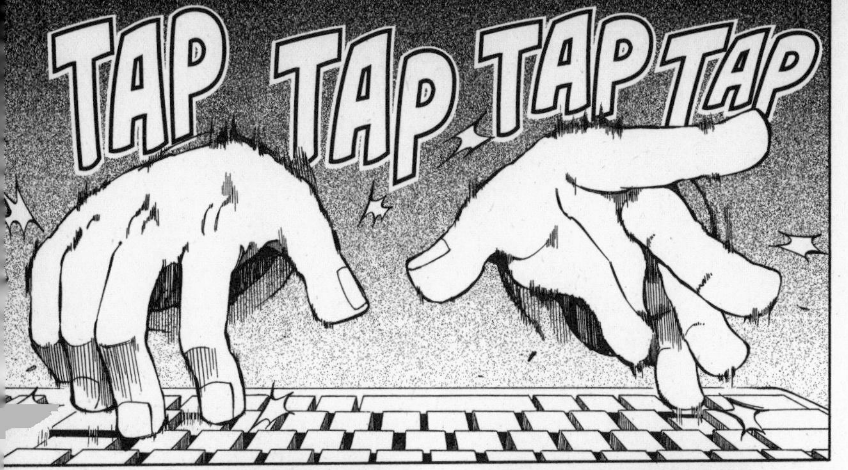
TAP TAP TAP TAP

HEH HEH...
TAP TAP

ALL RIGHT...IT SEEMS THEY FOUND THEY LOCATION OF GENRYU.
JUST AS PLANNED.
THEY HAVE NO IDEA THEY'RE BEING HACKED...
7th turn Reshuffle

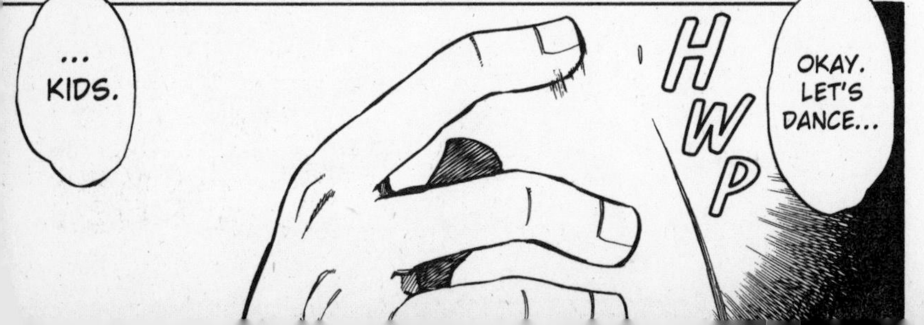
OKAY. LET'S DANCE...
HWP
... KIDS.

# 7th turn
# Reshuffle

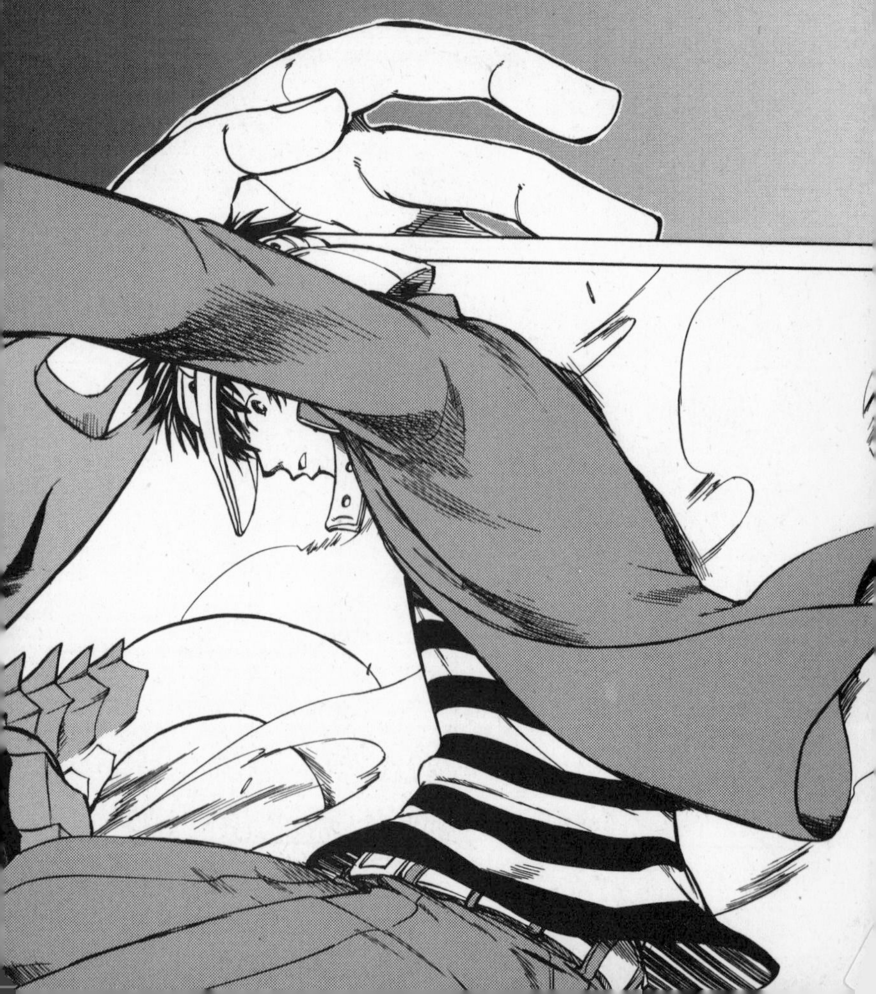

DRAGONIC
HEAVEN
BEGINS!!

ZHK
AMAZING.
THAT KID CALLED UP SO MUCH POWER.

READ THIS WAY

WAAAH

!

TAKUMI, ARE YOU OKAY?

UGH...

IT'S NO GOOD.

BUT ...
... DRAGON DRIVE...
... IS SO INTER-ESTING.
HMPH.
I DON'T KNOW WHAT TO DO WITH YOU.
AND DON'T GIVE ME THAT LOOK.
LISTEN! EVERYONE HAS A LIMIT!!
URGH ...
LISTEN TO ME, TAKUMI!
IF YOU DON'T LEARN THE DISCIPLINE TO CONTROL YOURSELF, YOU CAN NEVER BE TRULY STRONG...
BLAH
BLAH
BLAH
CUT IT OUT, RAIKOO.
YOUR NAGGING'S JUST MAKING ME SLEEPIER ...

SHP
!
TH
UK

DONK
OW!

SORRY, RAIKOO!
ROLL ROLL
I'LL LISTEN TO YOU! DON'T GET ANGRY!

HUH?
HEY!
RAI-KOO?

HURR ...

PEOPLE ...
WHOA!
VROOOOM
WHAT'S THIS CAR DOING HERE?
WAAAAH
HEY, MASTER, THE PROGRAM'S GOT A BUG.
WHAT THE...

Dragon Drive
Central Management Center

BEEEP
BEEEP
BEEEP
WE HAVE ERRORS IN THE SYSTEM!!
WHAT'S HAPPENING? I CAN'T USE MY COMPUTER!
THE SERVER'S CRASHED!!
THE SYSTEM IS BEING HIJACKED!

READ THIS WAY
Sapporo
Dragon Drive Center
RI-IN R
HEY, MASTER, WHAT EVENT IS THIS?
ERM ...
BUZZ
IT'S NOT AN EVENT. IT LOOKS LIKE A BREAK-DOWN.
DRAGON DRIVE
SAPPORO
THIS LOOKS BAD...
BZZ
Osaka
Dragon Drive Center
BUZZ
IT SAYS ...
... RI-IN.
BUZZ
BUZZ
KLUMP
DRAT THEM...
WHAT ARE THEY DOING?

Tokyo
Dragon Drive Center
KOIZUMI
GAME SHOP
WE HAVE ERRORS BREAKING OUT ON ALL THE SERVERS.
SORRY, TAKUMI AND BUNROKU. WE CAN'T CONTINUE.
I'M GONNA HIT THE EMERGENCY RESET.
KLUNK
TAKUMI YUKINO AND BUNROKU AZUMA: EMERGENCY RESET.
KLUNK
WAAAH
WAAAH

READ THIS WAY

KINDA ... LIKE ...

...SOME-THING PASSED THROUGH ME.

WHAT'RE YOU TALKING ABOUT?

...

OH.

WHAT?

SKREEEE

CRUNCH

WHAM

CRASH

WHAT?
BAM !
HEY! WAIT UP, GUYS! CALM DOWN!!
WAAH
TA-KUMI!
BOSS !!
VMMMM
WHOA ...

NO WAY!! WHAT HAPPENED?
GET THE COPS!! NO, AN AMBULANCE!! CALL AN AMBULANCE !!

WHAT'S GOING ON HERE?
!!
WHAT HAPPENED TO THAT BUILDING?

TA-KUMI ...
YEAH ...
I THINK ...
...SOME-THING **WEIRD** IS STARTING.

READ THIS WAY
I DON'T BELIEVE IT.
I MUST BE DREAMING.
ALL THE CARS ARE EMPTY.
MASTER, WE CAN'T GET THROUGH TO THE POLICE.
...
MASTER!
HEY, WHERE'S TAKUMI?
TA-KUMI?
HE WAS RIGHT HERE A MINUTE AGO.
BUT I CAN'T FIND HIM ANY-WHERE!
WHAT?
GAME SHOP
KOIZUMI
THE GUYS FROM THE DAICHI GANG ARE GONE, TOO!!
TA-KUMI! WHERE ARE YOU?

THERE ARE CAR ACCIDENTS ALL OVER THE PLACE...

THERE ARE NO PEOPLE!
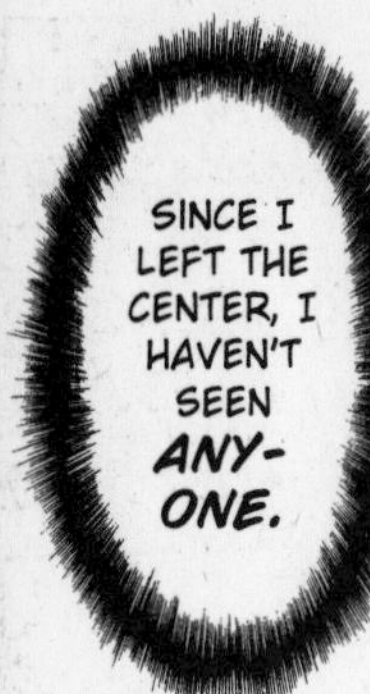
SINCE I LEFT THE CENTER, I HAVEN'T SEEN ANY-ONE.

WHERE DID EVERY-BODY GO?

TAK
TAKKA

SHF

HFF
HFF
HFF
HFF

HFF
HFF
HFF

YUKINO

MOM ...

HFF

HFF

HFF

READ THIS WAY

...
FSST
FSST
SHAAAAA

CLICK
FSST
CHAKKA
BDMP
BDMP
BDMP

SNIFF...
HELLO!
HUH?
WHO ARE YOU?
WAAAH!
DOOM
CAN I COME IN?
CLOMP
SOB
TOK TOK
EEEK! WAIT! WHO ARE YOU?
ARE YOU LOOKING FOR YOUR FAMILY, TAKUMI?
!
Y...
YOU'RE ...
REGRET-TABLY ...
...THEY ARE NO LONGER HERE.

FZZZT
WAAAAH!
I DON'T LIKE THIS! I WANNA GO HOME !!
HER NAME IS NEKO CHIHODA.
I FOUND HER HIDING IN THE PARK OVER THERE.
SNIFF
ER ...
UM ...
I'M TAKUMI YUKINO. NICE TO MEET YOU.
DON'T TRY TO SWEET-TALK ME! WHAT'S GOING ON?
LOB
THIS IS NO TIME FOR MANNERS!
I HATE YOU AND YOUR STUPID WEIRD HAT! STUPID! STUPID!
THWOK
BONK
CALM DOWN, NEKO.

WHEN I LEFT THE CENTER, THE STREETS WERE IN CHAOS!

WAAAH

THERE WAS NOBODY AROUND, AND THEN SOME WEIRDO **CHASED** ME!

I CAN'T STAND THIS...

THE CENTER?

WERE YOU AT A D.D. CENTER, TOO?

READ THIS WAY

AN EVIL ORGANIZATION CALLED ***RI-IN*** HAS TAKEN OVER THE DRAGON DRIVE SYSTEM...

REAL

VIRTUAL D-ZONE

...AND THEY'VE EXCHANGED THE PEOPLE ON EARTH WITH THE DRAGONS IN THE D-ZONE.

ARE... ARE MY PARENTS OKAY?
FOR NOW, YES.
BUT WE LOST CONTROL OF THE SYSTEM TO *RI-IN.*
THEY'RE LIKE HOSTAGES. WE CAN'T GET A CONNECTION FROM HERE.
SO HOW COME WE'RE HERE?
EVERY-ONE WHO WAS IN A D.D. CENTER STAYED ON EARTH.
D-Zone
D.D. Center
Shield
The Real World
IT WAS PROGRAMMED SO THAT PEOPLE IN THE CENTERS WOULD NOT BE EXCHANGED.
THEY CALL IT THE "BIG KIDNAPPER" PROGRAM...
WHAT?
YOU MEAN ...
...AND I CREATED IT.

RAI!!
WH...
WHAT WAS THAT?
BRR
BRR
VEE
EEEN
WE... WE'RE IN DANGER HERE...
RAI RAI RAIIII!!
TH... THAT'S...
...NOT A STUFFED ANIMAL?
RAIZO SAYS IT'S DANGER-OUS!!

RAI!

RAI!

WHEN AN ENEMY IS APPROACHING, HE ALWAYS FREAKS OUT!

I BET THAT WEIRDO CAME BACK!

LIGHTNING RAIZO

LV.1 AP 0 Pow 0

KER
BLAM
EEEEEK!

SMASSH

LIGHTNING DOKUDENPA
LV.2 AP 3400 Pow 1

THE DAMAGE TO THAT BUILDING...
...WAS DONE BY A DRAGON!!

IT... IT'S TRUE!
THERE'S A DRAGON IN THE REAL WORLD!!

WHERE'S THE OLD MAN?
HUH?
HE RAN OFF!!

WAM

!

READ THIS WAY
I'LL DISTRACT HIM. MAKE A RUN FOR IT!!
WHAT?
GRP
WAAH!
NO!
I CAN'T SURVIVE ON MY OWN!
MP
WU
TA-KUMI!!
CRUNCH

UGH ...
IF THE D-ZONE DRAGONS ARE IN THE REAL WORLD...
...DOES THAT MEAN YOU'RE HERE, TOO?
RAI...
...KOO ...
COME ON!
HERE I AM!

PLEASE!!

COME TO ME!

RAIKOO!!

RAARRR!!

RAIKOOO!!
ROAR!
KRAK
KRAK
TA-KUMI! HERE I AM!!
I...
...AM HERE!!!

THWAK

FZZT
FZZT
FZZT
RAIKOO!
COOL...

I CAN'T FIND THE OLD MAN.

SOB

SOB

MAYBE HE'S DEAD...

KLAK

HEY ...
WHAT'S GOING TO HAPPEN TO US?
SOB
SOB

9 RESHUFFLE The End

BY NAGI

Betrayal
RAI-KOO! TO-GETHER FOR-EVER!
YEAH! TA-KUMI!!
TINKLE
WHEW ...
THAT FELT GOOD!
W-C
RUB RUB
Raikoo card
DRIP
DRIP
EWW, GROSS! I CAN'T INPUT THIS CARD!
IT'S NO GOOD!
I'M SORRY!
BEEP BEEP
HUH?
TO THINK THAT IT WOULD END THIS WAY!!

Amazing developments! Breathtakingly dynamic!! Saken Theater's exciting special edition, part 2!!

IT'S STARTING.

ALL RIGHT, LET'S CONTINUE FROM LAST TIME...

...REVEALING OBO-CAT'S HIDING PLACES.

IS THAT RIGHT?

YEAH?

WELL, LET'S SEE THE ANSWERS.

IT'S JUST THAT...HOW CAN I SAY THIS?

WHEN I'M MAKING THIS FEATURE, THERE'S A GOOD CHANCE I'LL CUT MY HAND ON THE PAPER CUTTER...

TSK

YOU'RE TOO CLUMSY!!

JUST HAVE A LAUGH AT NUTTY, CLUMSY SAKEN!!

DO WHAT YOU WANT WITH ME.

FLUMP

YOU STILL LOVE YOURSELF.

YEAH...

QUITE A LOT...

ANYWAY.

OBO

VOLUME 5

STAGE 17: PAGE 34, FOURTH PANEL.

HEH HEH HEH... BUT IT'S STILL NOT ENOUGH...

STAGE 18...

DON'T TELL ME YOU FORGOT TO DRAW IT...

BRR BRR

Cat Lover

DRAGON DRIVE 5

STAGE 19: PAGE 119, FOURTH PANEL.

STAGE 20: PAGE 155, FIRST PANEL.
VOLUME 6
HEY!
STAGE 21: PAGE 36, FOURTH PANEL.
OPEN YOUR EYES!
STAGE 22: PAGE 56, FIFTH PANEL.
RGH!
STAGE 23...
UM...
HUH?
STAGE 24: PAGE 152, THIRD PANEL.
VOLUME 7
BOO!
STAGE 25: PAGE 38, SECOND PANEL.
STAGE 26: PAGE 82, THIRD PANEL.
RR
STAGE 27: PAGE 97, FOURTH PANEL.
WHEEP WHEEP
STAGE 28: PAGE 180, BOTTOM RIGHT PANEL.

## Heartwarming Saken Playhouse

# COMING NEXT VOLUME...

Takumi and his friends set out to learn what's happened to the people of Earth and how they can set things right. But the journey won't be easy, as our heroes are pursued by wild dragons, Ri-IN agents and fellow D-masters turned nasty. Fortunately, some old friends from the last Rikyu conflict are there to lend a hand...

***AVAILABLE IN OCTOBER 2008!***